Same Window 2 Different Views

Same Window 2 Different Views

Deluxe

Tyree Colbert

BlessingsThatProsper publishing

CONTENTS

2 | MAY 29TH 2006   7

3 | Sometimes   11

4 | April 27th, 2006   12

5 | Rainy Days   17

6 | Survivors Guilt   18

7 | Told Tyrell   20

8 | Myself   21

9 | How   23

10 | 2104   25

11 | To Be A Father   26

12 | Fighting   28

13 | I Know   30

CONTENTS

14 | Not Going 32

15 | Prelims 33

16 | Emotions 34

17 | Away 36

18 | Made Me 38

19 | Legacy Of Pride 39

20 | Standing 40

21 | Gain 41

22 | Living 42

photo insert 44

23 | Not A Baby 45

24 | Still 47

25 | Go Crazy 49

26 | Crazy Lil Nigga 51

27 | I Can't 52

28 | Taste 53

29 | Dear Bro   54

30 | Forever   55

31 | Brilliant   56

32 | Slow Days   58

33 | Dedication   59

34 | High school Musical   60

35 | Ree   61

36 | Mama Said   63

37 | Cover 2   64

38 | Far   65

39 | To Believe   67

40 | Toast   68

41 | I would Never   70

42 | Subject Matter   72

43 | Back When   74

44 | 351,000 Hours   76

CONTENTS

45 | Healing   78

JORDAN

I'm Tyree Colbert

17 years old from Kansas City, MO.

This book is a window into the window I look out of.

Family, death, loves, pain, betrayal

in my 16 years.

I'M J. COLBERT

I GUESS TO BE A FATHER, REAL LEADER AND MAN OF GOD

YOU HAVE TO FIGHT YOUR OWN DEMONS IN SILENCE WHILE

HELPING OTHERS FIGHT THEIR DEMONS OUT LOUD.

SOMETIMES YOU JUST WANT TO CRY, SCREAM &

BREAKDOWN BUT YOU CAN'T ALL EYES ARE ON YOU FOR STRENGTH.

YOU'RE THE VOICE OF REASON, THAT EVEN THO THINGS DON'T

MAKE SENSE THAT GOD HAS A HIGHER PURPOSE AND THAT

EVERYTHING IS MEANT.

MAY 29TH 2006

Birth of Tyree with the Wicks
This a story I'm always quicker to say
Not confident the magnitude of the events on
paper I could convey it was Monday.

Actually, Memorial Day. From the 28th since bout 8pm
Robin and I went to the hospitals 3 times but they
kept sending us home again & again
Talking 'bout oh it's just Braxton Hicks
Robin kept saying no if he not coming something
wrong y'all need to fix.

Us being 22 & 21 people could be real pricks
Like we didn't know shit they told us go home
Doctor face felt my spit
Hands balled up somebody was going get hit.

Robin saved me from making a bad situation worse I
can admit when she grabbed my arm and said come on let's split.

How bad it could of been long term has no limit.

It's bout 11am May 29th when we return home
exhaustion started to be shown.
Couldn't even make it upstairs laid down in the
living room on air mattresses I just blown
Soon as started to go in REM zone Robin woke
me to an uncontrolled groan.
I look she is on all fours
Focusing past her roars
Blood covering the floor
Like ocean water rushing the shores.
Flowing from her source
I scream "Don't move" frantically thinking best
action to take course.

Hello, this is 911 "My pregnant wife bleeding from
her vagina she 9 months please send ambulance fast."
I never knew how long 7 mins could last.

They arrive put her on a gurney covered her face
with oxygen mask sirens blazing we're headed to hospital
I'm holding her hand paramedic ask am I the baby father I said
"No I'm the husband"
He said "Well sir we may only be able to save one who
do you want to save?"
Processing what he said my heart started to cave
Frozen with no words eyes filling with tears couldn't
even try to brave seconds from reacting with anger
like "What the fuck you mean neither better not
go to their grave." Again protecting me from me Robin

removed the mask and said "My baby is who you save."
Come here" is what I was told
Placed my head on her chest
Rubbing my head saying "I ....No!!!... we need you at your best "
"J.Tyrell Colbert don't stress"
"God got us, everything going be alright"
Till don't know how she was comforting me in the middle of
a fight for her and our son's life.
We get to the hospital up the elevator
to labor & delivery we go.

Before the elevator could stop his head started to show.
Soon as we got in room, boom
my 3rd son was here safe from his mothers womb.
Robin and I embrace, praising the Lord for his grace.
They placed our son in her arms oh the pride on her face.
Then she said to me "Hold your son."
Soon as I got him in my arms it was like the
room spun. Robin coded, they rush to bring her back blood
she needed to get reloaded.
I held our son as I prayed.

Talking to God while looking at Tyree I wasn't afraid.
I knew God was great and God will let her awake.
Even as doctors started to state the amount of blood
she has lost was same as gun shot victim who paid
the ultimate cost.

Doctors looked with confusion
her opening her eyes wasn't an illusion May 29th 2006
was the day God showed the paramedics the doctors the

nurses he does exist.

J. Colbert

Sometimes

Sometimes I like dreaming more than I like being alive.
I haven't been the same since I got the news my
big brother died.
I don't know who's real anymore;
somehow, everybody eventually ends up switching sides.
Long live 3, long live Mud, shit, I miss the guys.
Feel like y'all should've never died.
Sometimes I break down,
then I realize I'm a king in this shit.
I gotta wear my crown.
Y'all can find that old Ree he
somewhere in the lost and found.
I don't really write for real,
but my pops said he loves my sound.

Tyree Colbert

April 27th, 2006

April 27th, 2006 is the day Robin (21) and I (22) said I do.
No ceremony; we were in our living room.
We said we didn't need a production to make our love true.
Tank top, basketball shorts, but you were proud to call
me your groom.
Already a lifetime of chaos we had been through, a lifetime
more together was all we could view.
With our third child, second together, in your womb,
who knew things would change so soon.
It was the 19th day of June;
life came causing catastrophic damage like a typhoon.
We were still in sync; we were still dancing to the
same tune.

Shortly after, I went on vacation like the National Lampoon.
As the head of the house, I messed up; I was a buffoon.
I made an ass out of you and me; you know I assumed.
It was the same demons from before; we beat so
many times, their bullshit we were immune.

Not being ready for new devils, our marriage put us
at new levels; lesson learned, never presume.

But, that mistake might have caused our doom.
The devil came as I was trying to be the head of
my home, through letters and over the phone
how opportune. The devil came dressed in the family costume.
Eventually, all the seeds we had planted that started to bloom
were now covered in gloom.

Next, you were drinking alcohol, something you swore
never to consume; upon my return home, we just
couldn't get back in tune.
As you battled your demons, the role of full-time father
I presumed.

We still didn't want to sign the papers, officially calling it
quits; the way we still loved one another made it hard to admit.
Eventually, we had to sign them and submit; then we all
took an irreplaceable, earth-shattering hit.
We both didn't like how the other handled it; before you
know, I'm doing some unbelievable, crazy shit.
I would've thought I lost it too.

I can omit with no conversation; you couldn't
understand; you let me know how you felt whenever you ranted.
I had a plan, despite all that; our healing had begun; priceless
moments in a short timespan.

You chasing me at break; you must have forgotten how fast I ran.
It was Thursday, April 25th; it was after midnight, so it

was Friday, the 26th, right? You were walking five feet
in front of me; I wanted to cry and
scream, tell you the shit wasn't what it seemed.
I was living in what felt like a bad dream, trying to get out
by any means.

If I told you I needed your help, you had my back; that I
could guarantee; listening to you cuss me out would've been
the only fee.

April 27th, 2019, would have been our anniversary of
year 13; sometime throughout the day, I began feeling
some type of way. My heart started to weigh;
Lil Tyrell running, telling me,
still in my head on replay.
I became stuck in a daze, hoping at any moment he was
going to rephrase; trying to gather myself so the reality
of his words I can face; knowing I can't break down,
gotta be strong for the kids was the case.

I ask him who called you; I said, "Your cousin who?
You sure it's true? Your grandma, your auntie, your
uncle would have called to make sure y'all knew."
We head out the door, troubled down to our core,
driving to the hospital, not sure what we're in for.
We run into the ER, demanding to know where you
are; answer our questions they refuse, then take us
to this little room.

The clergy walks in; I already know the news; I
grab Ty, making sure he doesn't get loose.

He begins screaming, "Momma"; the clergy looks
confused; he said, "I thought all her immediate family
just left and were aware; I said, "Impossible; this the oldest
of her four kids right here."

At that moment, after already nobody called your
children that you carried and pushed out, I refused
to speak it out my mouth; for the first time, I gave your
family the benefit of the doubt.
Praying they would not do our babies wrong, knowing
your death would affect them lifelong.
So I played the background, going along to get along,
just staying close enough to keep our babies strong.
Then with money involved, I knew what time they were
going to be on; they would try to have some kind of
issues with me to justify them doing our babies wrong.
Simple people, plans, and character are feeble; how I called
every move they did before they did it.
Why I refused to get in the mud with them and sling shit.
A girl your sister tried to hook me up with for like a
double date; your sister wanted Jerry as a mate.
Jerry and I kept saying naw, we straight.
Before our divorce was even final, let's get that established
first; so when I heard they started lying, saying I was smacking
the same girl on the ass at your funeral outside the church,
I laughed because I knew it would only get worse.
Then Lil Ty, who was on your lease, after
three weeks of your sister stalling, he had the
office let him in your place so he can get some peace.
Again, the lady in the office only let him in
because she takes rides on my piece.

Took what he wanted of him and his siblings'
stuff, and they try to call the police. Police
told them this bullshit they need to cease.
When they gave your kids beds & furniture
away to people on the streets, then Lil Ty dropped
the release. Let everybody know your
sister got over 250K from your Ford.

J. Colbert

Rainy Days

It was a lot of rainy days just looking for clear weather,
Long live my brothers, wish y'all could've
trapped forever. Just want me and my mom to be back
together, Them days were better, Tyi'san, missing you hella.
She can't wait till she can fit into your sweater,
No care about how old I get, I'll be your baby forever.
Without your side of the family, we've been a lot better,
Used to hate showing you my homework 'cause
you were a key spell checker.
I remember the way I used to mess up on the headers,
I'll be with you soon,
We gonna be laying in them big cloud beds together.

Tyree Colbert.

Survivors Guilt

My son is nineteen,
I can't explain what all he's seen
before he was even a teen.
None of the pain he has endured
was foreseen.

He's at college out of state, a whole new scene.
Excelling, he's on the list made by the dean,
past behind him it would seem.
Now he's got survivors guilt on top
of his anxiety & PTSD.

Never was in armed forces fighting a
war overseas. Not the lone survivor of a tragic
accident or some gunman's shooting spree.
Just got out of a community where
death or prison only future you could guarantee.
For a black male truthfully, family and friends
that were family, memories condensed just to a eulogy.

Knowing they could've been great if given the
opportunity are the thoughts he has continuously.
Still not placing his life above theirs humbly,
Honestly, it's tragically a beautifully ugly mentally.

J. Colbert

Told Tyrell

Told Tyrell keep his head up 'cause I remember
folding what we called a bed up,
My goal always get my bread up.
Just 'cause they your blood,
Don't mean they give a fuck.
In my city you gotta keep iron, but it's not for put
everyone tryna be on my team 'cause
I'm balling they all cut.

Tyree Colbert.

8

Myself

In competition with myself in 5 years,
I know how I'ma build generational wealth.
Can't compare me to the average 16-year-old,
They ain't felt the pain I felt.
All the cards I was dealt until
People hear my story, their hearts start to melt.
Like "Young man, you walk with all this on your belt."
Know how it feel to lose my pops to my system,
'Cause he will never tell.
I'm Tyree mentally, I'll probably never find the true me.
Looked up my name and them words don't define me.
Shout out my godmother Shauna 'cause when I
Look in her eyes I see a true G.
Know if I ever need, she gon' be able to take care of me.
When she made that pact with my mom, she
Said your babies is my babies.
She stood on it harder than her own
Family, this life crazy.
I don't write for real but when I do it get me closer

with Lil Mudbaby.

Tyree Colbert.

9

How

The Therapist said
"To help with my ptsd have to let go
of stuff in my head"
I said "Stuff like what?"
Get awaken to a knock at the door and
Them telling me get around the corner quick
your son might be dead."
"Or I get a call to the hospital I go see my
nephew's side of his face is mangled with a
hole where his eye used to be."
"How do I let go?"
Please let me know.
Close friend like family gets shot in
the hospital parking lot.
Praying for good news from the screams of the
crowd I already knew the news.
Too many times laughing playing house full of cheer
Then next thing I know my son running in the room
telling me a parents worse fear About his peer

I can go on & on
Doc please tell me how I let that kind of stuff go.
Do you have a magic wand?
I went from burying peers my age
to now helping bury my kids peers I helped raise.
Watching my kids suffer pain I can't heal
Knowing exactly how they feel.
When I should of been watching "All dogs go to heaven"
I was too busy
praying that all my dogs go to heaven.
Still a product of society
So much trauma therapist don't even know how to treat me

J. Colbert

2104

2,104 days since I got to talk to my big brother,
I know you okay 'cause God sent you my mother.
I cry all the time, really wish we left with each other,
Really had the best big brother in the world,
Can't compare him to no other.
Hella shit changed the way me and Tyrell been living.
You would be happy 'cause we been turnt.
My brother Tyrell getting money out in Houston,
I'm still in high school doing what I be doing.
But that money talk, we talking it real fluent.
I know you was laughing at me and Tyrell my
freshman year 'cause we stayed truent.
A lot of shit ain't the same, wish I
Could call you and get into it.

Tyree Colbert.

To Be A Father

I guess To be a father, real leader and man of God
you have to fight your own demons in silence While
helping others fight their demons out loud.
Sometimes you just want to cry, scream &
breakdown but you can't All eyes are on you for strength.
You're the voice of reason, that even tho things don't
make sense that God has a higher purpose and that
everything is meant.
Even tho mentally your spent You have to uplift
You have to make others believe So they can achieve
Hiding your pain so no one can see.
I do all this while dealing with one bad decision
that has permanently impaired my vision.
When all the social media "rip" post & phone calls stopped
This pain down to my soul this hole in my heart this void
to my life didn't stop.
The hole the pain actually grows as every hour, minute and
second pass on the clock So at times I find it therapeutic
To escape my reality in these pharmaceutics.

I don't want to hear "Its all part of God's plan."
You didn't have to stand where I stood and watch
as they put your oldest son in a bag then place him the back
of a coroners van.
I'm just a man so I cant see how that image was a part of some
great plan Stop telling me "It's okay it's Gods Work."
When every time I want to have a conversation with my son I
have to go and talk to dirt So your telling me then Gods
work is Hurt.
Yes I still believe in God Yes I'm strong
This not about my strength I know how to hold on.
The struggle everyday is figuring out how I carry on.
I have a beautiful family I'm very blessed
But I'm also depressed Can you blame me.

J. Colbert

12

Fighting

Been fighting demons since Shawn didn't
come home.
In my city, young niggas wanna score
but not in the end zone.
Wish Shawn could just phone home.
My mind it roams.
Just want Blessing to play sports, he
big enough to make it to the Super Dome.
All the pain I seen, you would think
I was grown.
But, that's what my town did to me, it's
hard to be Ree.
Y'all couldn't handle what I see.
When I tell my stories, I don't want people
to cry for me.
Just want 'em to take their shit to the chin
like a G.
'Cause y'all wouldn't handle walking with me.

Tyree Colbert.

I Know

I know I'm not supposed to question God
I'm staring up to the Sky
Oh My God
I need to know why.
I can't relax everyday I'm tense
Nothing makes sense.
My heart has an everlasting stain
that is full of pain.
Most days it's hard for me to get out of bed
Not wanting to deal with the harsh reality of facing
another day knowing my son is dead.
Even when i have good moments and start smile
I begin feeling guilty after a while.
How am I to have joy when my son is gone forever
16 years old so many memories and experiences I will
get to share with him never.
I know I'm not supposed to question God
But I'm staring up to the sky
Oh My Dear God

I need to know why.

J. Colbert

Not Going

One day, I wanna be bigger than Big Pun,
Do this poetry thing for fun.
I was taught to be a man without a gun,
But I ain't going for none.
Y'all don't know how it feels to be
Robin's youngest son,
I ain't going for none.
Imma be real to my people until my time is done,
And all my people won.
Just want my life to lighten up like the sun,
Pops said your life just begun.
Get hot streaks with my poetry so I just go on a run.
Not the one to cross, so move with caution.

Tyree Colbert.

Prelims

My 16-year-old son asked me how many
funerals have I had to attend.
I said "Why?"
He said "Wondering if it will ever end."
Looking to the sky.
I slowly reply
"It never ends unless you
run out of family & friends
or you win."
"He said what do you mean win?"
A ticket to heaven with no sin.
That's when your life really begins
This is here just the prelims.

J. Colbert

Emotions

They asking too many questions
I feel like I'm talking to the narcs.
Ever since Shawn and my mom died scared of cars
Some times I just cry tears out of nowhere
'Cause I'm emotionally scarred.
Really wish I wasn't having to say "Free Nell"
And "Free Zay" instead of "Do it for 3"
And "Do it for Zay."
I just hope I'm at peace wit myself when
It's my last day.
Got hella pride but nah I'm not gay
Pops telling me turn my music off 'cause I keep playing
We all gotta leave sum day.
Got hella pride but nah I'm not gay
Pops telling me turn my music off 'cause I keep playing
We all gotta leave sum day.
'Cause I know we do 'cause I seen people I was
The closest with pass away.

Tyree Colbert.

Away

Once you start thinking you can't quit it's like crack
Before you know it your thoughts start to determine
how you act.

Once you start to look at the world and really start to focus in
You start to notice our world goes round by sin.
So I live to die and die to live again
But because of my sins will my life never end.
The good ones always die first
Is that because they already earned their wings and get
to ride in that beautiful black Hearst.

What if we already living in hell
But too blind and foolish to tell.
Is that because our wisdom is little to none
Because we sleep when we're tired even tho sleep is deaths
begotten son.

When I smoke they say I'm smoking my life away

What if I'm just smoking away my chance to fly away.
I do what I'm supposed too and go to church
There I see the most hypocrites and fornicators so you
know that starts to hurt.

I only have one fear for that day I get away from here
Will I make it to a place where I no longer shed a tear.

J.Colbert

Made Me

That shit made me cry seen niggas closer
than loves ones die.
Sad reality this is not the American dream.
I put a smile on my face cause if I told you
what I seen
you would ask why is he not so mean.
Cause I'm young and focused on tryna
get green.
I'm a future success story I can't be fein.

Tyree Colbert.

Legacy Of Pride

I don't war with men,
My battles are won within.
I can live a hundred years
And nobody know I was here, that's a fear.
Not just any attention, respect.
Integrity and honor or don't mention
A legacy of pride, God my guide.
If I fail along the ride, the why
Won't be I didn't try.
I give my all
So my descendants walk tall.

J. Colbert

20 |

Standing

They shooting in the malls from my mom's
side I don't get a call.
I don't like the summer, I fuck with the fall.
Just want me and my guys to be rich
So we can ball.
Young nigga but I stand on business,
you would think I Was tall.

Tyree Colbert.

Gain

They pronounced my brother dead on the scene
its crazy aunt Dorinda can see
but can't see a thing.
fell in love with writing poetry I gotta give my first
book a ring.
I taught all 5 of my lil sisters find love cause all niggas
wanna do is ping.
was taught if the cops ask you ain't seen a thing love my
mama she taught me if I work hard enough I can get anything.
I'm making money off typing my pain
mama all the L's you taught me charge it to the game.
Sick Mud died cause he was gone be in the Rock and Roll
Hall Of Fame.
Mama your baby ain't the same all he feel is pain,
but he still tryna focus and change the game.
Cause your baby different he got nothing to lose but all to gain.

Tyree Colbert.

Living

Pops tryna show me it's something to live for in this life.
I'm already gone feel like died twice.
I see my people face when I close my eyes
days before my sophomore year I seen one of my
brothers die.
So numb to losing people I don't how to cry
they at the end of line you get the pie.
But, I don't want slice don't live in America
cause you don't get no
rights.
Shawn taught how to fight before he lost his life that's
why wit this shit
I live for the day cause it could be my last night tonight.

Tyree Colbert.

Not A Baby

You playing Roblox I'm rolling blocks.
You was on the step and drill team
While I was stepping and drilling shit with my team.
You play the drums for fun
I play with drums for my funds.
You need a night light to go to sleep
I need something next to me
that will light the night up to go to sleep.
All the young niggas know is creep long
live mud don't hit this street.
Cause he still ah make the car beep all the sneak
disses I peep.
Own family talking crazy they must've
forgot who raised me.
Cause I'll get to camping outside they shi.
I'm grown now I am not that lil baby
I just wanna get rich and feel like Tay B.
young nigga wit a bag it's hard to play me.

Tyree Colbert.

Still

You playing Roblox I'm rolling blocks.
You was on the step and drill team
While I was stepping and drilling shit with my team.
You play the drums for fun
I play with drums for my funds.
You need a night light to go to sleep
I need something next to me
that will light the night up to go to sleep.
All the young niggas know is creep long
live mud don't hit this street.
Cause he still ah make the car beep all the sneak
disses I peep.
Own family talking crazy they must've
forgot who raised me.
Cause I'll get to camping outside they shi.
I'm grown now I am not that lil baby
I just wanna get rich and feel like Tay B.
young nigga wit a bag it's hard to play me.

Tyree Colbert.

25 |

Go Crazy

Robin Youngest son Rez gone.
All I can do is talk to his mom.
Bro they say I'm different cause my wicks.
But I was the same with a Fro
lost my guys young sad we can't grow old.
don't put my trust in people cause in the end they fold or told.
Dissing the dead without doing it to em is real bold internet
gangsters them IG lives the one who told.
The boys smart they seeing thru that weak ass code.
Just wanna spend time with lil Phoenix.
She turns my sad face into a face that glows
really just like to be alone don't care about the hoes.
Rough road I've traveled but it made me lost a lot
so a part of that made me crazy.
Not good at school but good with guns.
So I'm thinking about the navy
I mind the business that pays me.
Cause if I've worried about others my mind would go crazy.

Tyree Colbert.

Crazy Lil Nigga

Crazy lil nigga I get it from my mama
after you died it was all drama.
They're my family but I'll pop em
the way your brother keep getting shot idk
if that would stop em.
Your baby turnt now I'm crazy in the head.
I know I'm gone be ok every time it go down
Your sister she's the king of my family.
I'll shot at her right now.
They be ducking I don't never see em in town
mama you was the real queen I hope gave you
that crown in heaven now.

Tyree Colbert.

I Can't

I can't even cry no more
I don't even ask why no more
I cant even grieve no more
I don't even look to the sky no more
I only got two questions
What's the lesson?
Did they know today
Was the day
They would fly
With the One who eye
Is on the sparrow ?

J. Colbert

Taste

Blessing and prosper lost a sibling before
they was born.
That's why I make sure I stay safe.
Cause I can't let someone send shots at what prosper
calls" Tyree loving face"'
Streets ain't where you wanna be
you could know who killed your homie the police
will label it a close case.
I cry every time on the inside when they tell me you have
your big brothers face.
Cause I been running all my life from that pain I gotta face.
With this poetry shit I'm running tryna find
someone to match my pace
this just my first book aka a taste.

Tyree Colbert.

Dear Bro

I be missing my brother.
like damn why we have to separate from each other.
I'll give it all up for call with each other
but you up there with my mother.
Still wish we could be with each other.
It be crazy cause I look back cause we was just right
with each other.
You got a lil brother name blessing weird y'all ain't
get to meet each other.
Everyday I think why we couldn't just due the rest of
life with each other.

Tyree Colbert.

Forever

Pops answering a lot scam likely because uncle Sam.
Been getting moved a lot he been
from the bottom of the map to the top.
Move smart cause I watched the wire
I know it's easy to kill someone if you get the drop.
Lived a long life for a 16 year old never once met a good cop.
I was raised on we walk in together we walk out together.
Quick on my feet I'm bout as light as a feather.
Free all my friends who fell victim to the streets.
Sitting in the house like a dog cause the bracelet around
they leg we call tether.
I miss all my friends who passed but as long as I'm here
y'all spirits live forever.

Tyree Colbert.

Brilliant

So brilliant, values just insignificant
Preconditioned Mentally imprisoned impaired vision
Never given the equipment.
To see beyond what they know
Unable to grow.
Take the lid off box see beyond those 10 blocks
regardless how orthodox.
Too many already lost.
This to accost.
Those born behind enemy lines Lineage familiar to mines.
Whose power constantly declines Even In these times.
Following blueprints from Willie's designs
our community the victim to our crimes.
Infatuated by that that shines
Missing the signs.
We in a war attacks at our stores.
Consumed with battle of each other
They're able to walk up to kill our mother.
Who can't conquer a nation divided

Especially a nation using the mindset their enemy provided.
We must understand
Moving pass the past to make a stand.
To be a ManFor our descendants can have a different plan.

J. Colbert

Slow Days

I been having too many slow days
Going make me go back to my old.
Ways niggas flooding the town with bullshit
Tell my nothin to lose boys go take your shit.
Hit the highway
Go to a small town eat a full entree.
I'm not bout to play
Get you number chasing niggas out da way.
It's quality over quantity
Y'all only in this life partially.
9 to 5 what u count on constantly I count on 9 to 5 partially.
This here is my career, I hold it near & dear.
Honestly will be the death of me, possibly.

Tyree Colbert.

Dedication

Dedicated To
My Mother Robin Colbert
Love You Always & Miss You Dearly.
Dedicated to My Big brother
DaSean Colbert (Shawn).
Forever Shawn's World.
Dedicated to all my bro/friends.
I'm going rep to my last breath.

Tyree Colbert.

High school Musical

The view of my city is different from the look
they give on the news.
We losing people every day where I go to school.
They showing Pembroke Hill and Staley not showing how
Charles died one day after we got out of school.
Not explaining we got clear backpacks cause they
know kids got their tools at the school for school.
Round here them the rules.
Cause if you get caught without it they gonna fill you up.
I'm not talking about like the way you fill your cup.
My knuckles bruised.
I keep punching walls when I get bad news.
I hate to show the other side of Rec.
Yes, I feel I can win any fight cause I was fighting with me.

Tyree Colbert

35

Ree

I try so hard to understand people just for them to not
understand Ree.
Will anyone care when it's "Rest in Peace, Ree"?
Used to sit on the porch at 9013,
Wondering what I would be, now people can Google me.
I do this for that 10-year-old who lost his big brother and
the future he couldn't see.
Now you're graduating, I do this for Shawny but also for me.
At first, I ain't wanna walk,
But me and Pops had a talk,
"God brought you all the way here, do it for you and walk
across."
The 4 years I had in high school were different,
The kid that the teachers always said was missing, but you can
ask,
made my grades no different,
Till I took a 6-month break, went on a trip, and saw
a different vision.
Told Tyrell, tryna make sure my kids won't

experience the shit we lived in,
Cause a lot of people trapped in the KC mind, but I realized
this shit is far, far different from regular.

Tyree Colbert.

Mama Said

I'm working this Easter, Mama, you ain't dressing me, it's
all real s***, weird as hell,
When you grow up, you see that what they
were saying as a kid is so real.
Mama, I'll never be ashamed of who I am, 'cause you said
always be you and keep it real,
Same reason I can't hold my tongue for real.
I went to prom with bands 'cause senior year you
were focused on that, you were finna have Lil Tyrell.
RIP Aunt Dorinda, she got to see her 2 sons come home
from sentences on God's will,
That's why I keep faith for real.
Other people told my mama they got us and didn't keep it real,
So no, I wouldn't be mad if that junkie OD on a fentanyl pill.

Tyree Colbert.

Cover 2

Crazy, I played safety in middle school, but my safety's something
I really never cared about, 'Cause I ain't been feeling safe mentally
since Shawn left me to protect the house.
A year ago today, almost killed myself today,
I'm customizing this stow for graduation,
You don't always see the lesson when something first
happens, You gotta be patient.
I can get around my city with no GPS, a real Kansas City native
That got it off the pavement and focused on comma chasing
and making sure the youth not having court cases.

Tyree Colbert.

Far

Syrup sandwiches not tasting the same, prolly
'cause it reminds me of pain.
Sean not here no more, that shit's lame,
Waking up folding the floor,
No matter how much money you get, you're
not supposed to change.
Why ask how you are if you know my mama's gone?
Yo baby miss sitting next to you while you played cards,
Mama, you can talk yo shit 'cause even though I said I
never would, I been drinking hard.
I made amends, only thing I can blame you for is my
fear of driving cars.
But, I know you got me through them nights when
I was being a shooting star.
They ain't think I would finish school, my high-school
years were bizarre,
But in short due time if God allows, I'mma have 'em
saying "how he make it that far?"

Tyree Colbert.

39

To Believe

Many people told me I couldn't, but I knew
y'all believed in me, no matter where y'all were.
It was a long four years in high school,
but I did it for y'all.
But I'm still not done, I'mma have fun
The whole month of May 'cause Robin's youngest son
is making it to 18.
Shout out to them older members who say "stay out the way"
And just keep your head.
But I been doing that ever since I was walking on the canal,
smoking woods with Von.
Wicks long, focused on having seven different incomes,
I wish Robin could see her son.
Don't ask about what my mama's side did for
me 'cause this is not my pops talking.
On my dead momma, they ain't did nothing for me.

Tyree Colbert.

40

Toast

Toast to that!
I've seen Murda and Killa accusations remove OJ
from a place of grace, And then I've seen Murda and Killa
returning him to a place of
grace before he left this place. Toast to that!
I've seen my aunt Dorinda, blind and all, wait almost 30
years to see both her boys free, And after that, she was
able to go home at peace, so I guess she really could see.
Toast to that!
I've seen in 2016 news reporters come to my house to
report on the death of my son, Nowadays, reporters are
pulling up to the house to report how we're them ones.
Toast to that!
I've seen Claudette Colvin finally get some national recognition,
there went another mention to help bring attention. Toast to that!
I've seen, for once, only punishment wasn't just
becoming unemployed, after all the lives they destroyed.
Actually got justice for Floyd.
Toast to that!

I've seen myself, a Black man at 22 with three sons,
Seen as just another high school dropout by some.
Now them three sons, All graduated high school...
One at semester
and one posthumous, Even after his life on earth was done.
Toast to that!
I've seen my daughter try to un-alive herself, Nowadays, she's
preaching sermons from the pulpit 'bout God's wealth.

Toast to that!

J. Colbert

I would Never

Woman said, "I would never,"
I said, "we can agree to disagree,
But at least take the time to listen to me."
She said, "I'll listen, regardless what you say, I still would never."
I replied, "However,
We come from places with two different types of weather.
You come from blue skies,
With the high of 85,
A nice place to live life.
I come from scattered heavy metal showers; it's always
the forecast.
In the blistering cold, it can turn to 110 degrees real fast.
You come from where kids go outside to enjoy the nice scenery,
I come from where kids go outside carrying heavy machinery.
I'm not saying I'm not going be where you at one day,
Right now, though, this is where I stay.
I'm going to get my better day,
Somehow, someway.
In between time, this is the play,

For the world I live in,
Dealing with the evil of men.
You would never... Well, I would have never thought a war zone
would be where I'd be raising my kids up in.
It doesn't make national news around here when a teen gets shot,
Stepping off the bus at his bus stop;
Where you're from, the whole world would stop.
So, I have to play the odds,
Not the type of odds you're playing at the casino on slots.
It's life or death, freedom or prison,
This is what you call nonfiction.
I teach all my kids how to pray,
That the Bible is the only way to survival.
So, I had to say,
I know things can always go either way,
But the odds I must play,
On where I would rather stand,
Visiting room or watching the door to a casket slam.
So see, just like you, it was never my plan
To put a gun in my son's hand."

J. Colbert

Subject Matter

Subject matter,
Subject matter,
Subject matter,
What does it matter?
People only wanna hear the latter,
Don't wanna hear what it takes to climb the ladder.
Everybody wants the glory
Without having to live the story,
Feeding yourself
With materialistic wealth
Is bad for your health,
Like being pro-life but you support the death penalty,
Make that make sense to me.
The hypocrisy
Of this so-called democracy,
These are the people who make the policy,
And we wonder what's wrong with our economy.
These man-made titles
Got the people worshiping false idols,

Instead of reading their Bible.

Subject matter,
Subject matter,
Subject matter,
What does it matter?
People only wanna hear the latter,
Don't wanna hear what it takes to
climb the ladder.

J. Colbert

Back When

Back around '96
Before chill and Netflix
This is how I was pulling up on chicks
Before X Games
I was on the cement, popping wheelies to go
play my ex game.
Hey, well at least that's what we would say
No Subway Surfer but Subway did play
This little game we'd play
Might have had on a Cross Colours fit
I was the original CrossFit
Just to get a whiff of that slit
I would do all kinds of shit
Wish I could have seen my mile split
Running from a dog while hopping a fence
Hiding in closets, jumping out windows, fathers chasing me,
real-life suspense
Before Uber, 5 dollars in gas money would get the
older boys in the hood

To drop me off
Blasting "Boyz n the Hood"
They would make sure I was good
Before they took off
From 2Pac, Too Short, E40, 8Ball & MJG, Ghetto Boys & UGK,
a lot of game was taught
Over no skirt, no war should be fought
If you're from that cloth
So that lifestyle is what I sought
Living my best life is what I thought
For a 7th grader
Life couldn't get any greater.

J. Colbert

351,000 Hours

Sky is the limit
So I relax on a rooftop
The city is my backdrop
Not a bad boy but I can't stop
Won't stop
On my way to the top
Like Mufasa, this all belongs to me
As far as the eye can see
I've never been the norm
They will change the rules to get me to perform
Always the star of the show
Only poet you know
Had girls fighting at the high school talent show
Then hit the stage at Missouri Western State
Before niggas were woke, I was already awake
First got published in '88
Nothing's been overnight, let's get that straight
For a book of stamps, I would have sold you a poem in the pen
Now Sen

Is using my books of poems to minister to men
In the pen
I'm Him
Independent publishing company with international sales
I'm Him
Two of my kids got two books published a piece
Letting their testimonies bring others peace
I'm him
Ask about me
Then ask about me again
I'm not just a poet
I'm the poets' poet
Now go tell a friend.

J. Colbert

Healing

Old head had Said.
"Damn Ty you a cold piece of work,
You write poems you know will hurt."
I said "Well that's how healing works."
That's the perks of my work.

J. Colbert